BUILDING ON STRENGTH (BoS)

BUILDING ON STRENGTH (BoS)

Constructive Change for Nonprofit Organizations

Building from Strength Instead of Uncovering Weakness

Introduction and Workbook

Will Phillips and Mary Case

Qm^2: Quality Management To A Higher Power

BUILDING ON STRENGTH (BOS)
CONSTRUCTIVE CHANGE FOR NONPROFIT ORGANIZATIONS

iUniverse books may be ordered through booksellers or by contacting:

iUniverse
1663 Liberty Drive
Bloomington, IN 47403
www.iuniverse.com
844-349-9409

Because of the dynamic nature of the Internet, any web addresses or links contained in this book may have changed since publication and may no longer be valid. The views expressed in this work are solely those of the author and do not necessarily reflect the views of the publisher, and the publisher hereby disclaims any responsibility for them.

Copies of this book may be purchased at www.qm2.org or at www.iUniverse.com

Any people depicted in stock imagery provided by Getty Images are models, and such images are being used for illustrative purposes only.
Certain stock imagery © Getty Images.

ISBN: 978-0-5952-7744-5 (sc)

Print information available on the last page.

iUniverse rev. date: 10/11/2023

Contents

Introduction:

Most nonprofits have at their core the concept of a better world: healthy people; educated, inspired children; vibrant communities; esthetically pleasing environments. Most nonprofit practitioners have begun their work because of a passion for change—wanting to make the world a better place. So, we notice the issue—a historic building in the path of a wrecking ball, people without a place to call home, survivors of grim medical diagnoses, trash-strewn lots in our neighborhoods. Whatever the challenge, throughout our history, people step up to improve the situation.

In making these improvements, we frequently foster divisiveness in our organizations and communities by announcing what's wrong and commencing to fix it. Some people resist our proposals because they have a legitimate stake in the status quo, they don't like the proposed change, or they have little faith in the creation of a better world. We sometimes let our own fear and self-doubt impede our personal progress because the proponents of the status quo remind us of potential negative consequences.

In part because nonprofit leaders focus on noble causes, they may forget to create an effective organization. Nonprofits often adapt diluted or faddish change philosophies a decade after introduction in the for-profit world. By that time, the overall environment has shifted enough that the philosophy and associated techniques of change rarely deliver the rewards business may have reaped.

The military first formalized hierarchical organizations. The military model became the industrial model to run factories as people moved from farm and cottage industries to factory floors during the Industrial Revolution. This machine-like model replicates the factory floor and is based on span of control, job descriptions, reporting relationships and chain of command. This model treats people as inter-changeable parts and treats work as linear and sequential with delineated boundaries. Improvements are made by identifying problems and fixing them. The military-industrial model did a reasonable job of putting the hands and backs of farmers to work on the assembly line. The line itself, designed by management, embodied the manufacturing knowledge. Laborers were not expected to think. The industrial model saw workers as brawn, not brains valued for knowledge and judgment.

During the past fifty years, we've moved into a knowledge economy, yet most non-profits continue to use the hierarchical industrial model as the basis of organizing knowledge workers. Strangely, large museums and symphonies, industries where knowledge is the currency of production, remain bastions of hierarchy and authority. Modern education and communication systems exponentially enhance the individual's capacities to contribute to the organization. Human beings have extraordinary capacity to learn, to change, to initiate, to adapt, to collaborate and to manage stress. The hierarchical organization severely limits these capacities. In the industrial model, organizations improve by identifying and solving problems. Many small to mid-sized corporations have learned to be nimble and integrated, and to optimize the contributions of knowledge workers. The challenge is to let go of our life-long exposure to the industrial model beginning with the idea of the tough, hard-nosed, industrial magnate surrounded by loyal, obedient followers.

This book introduces a concept currently still residing mostly in academic research and organizational design journals, where most business change philosophies begin. So, we invite you to discover something very new and powerful, and we believe a natural fit to the nonprofit environment.

We must become the change we want to see.
Mahatma Gandhi

You can use BoS methods to:

- Build communities that work
- Lead change with reduced resistance
- Think and plan strategically
- Build focus for change
- Evaluate programs and services
- Energize board or staff retreats
- Make a real difference on diversity issues
- Manage your own life.

Building on Strength (BoS) History:

Building on Strength is a whole cloth, woven of several threads. Humans have a predilection to improve, tinker, change all sorts of things for the better. Fundamentally, BoS asks you to move away from seeking what's wrong in the world and fixing it and moving toward highlighting what's right and building upon it.

As a grad student at Case Western Reserve University in 1980, David Cooperrider and his professor, Suresh Srivastva, began to study the Cleveland Clinic. The Clinic operated with a high degree of cooperation, innovation, and egalitarian governance. Srivastva suggested that Cooperrider study the conditions that created and sustained this environment. Cooperrider and his colleagues have served as both a focus and a driving force in what has come to be known as Appreciative Inquiry (AI).

Finding problems and fixing them has also been the dominating force in individual development. When Martin E. Seligman became President of the American Psychological Association in 1996, he commented that psychological journals had published 45,000 articles in thirty years on depression, but only 400 on joy. His comment directly reflects organizational problem solving techniques, applied to individuals: to get better, find the problems and fix them.

A contrasting view arose in the 1960s, pioneered by John C. Crystal and Richard Nelsen Bolles. Crystal and Bolles, great icons of modern career and life planning, rejected the concept that individuals could not enter and succeed in fields where they did not have typical or traditional training and experience. Instead, they helped individuals identify past successes and extract the transportable skills, talents, and knowledge. With this understanding, literally hundreds of thousands of people built upon their experience and extended into a vast array of new careers.

Over the past two decades, Marvin Weisbord and Sandra Janoff have led an international movement to find common agreements in communities. Providing techniques to throw light on the common ground that people already agree upon, Future Searches, as the technique is called, have led polarized communities all over the globe to achieve peacefully and effectively what problems solving techniques could not do.

Recent research by the Gallup people, led by Marcus Buckingham and Curt Coffman, mined interviews with over 80,000 managers in more than 400 organizations, and encapsulated the mantra of great managers:

> *People don't change that much.*
> *Don't waste time trying to put in what was left out.*
> *Try to draw out what was left in.*
> *That's hard enough.*

Building on Strength (BoS) assumes that in every life, every organization, every community, some things work better than others. Identifying what works and building from it allows you, your organization and your community to launch new initiatives from a positive foundation already in place, thereby avoiding resistance. By Building on Strength, you largely eliminate resistance to change.

BoS lets go of traditional problem-solving methods. It's radical. It asks what works, rather than what doesn't. Rather than looking for problems (you'll find them), BoS looks for the best in the issue, and describes the future based on demonstrated successes. We leave it to you to confirm our enthusiasm. We think you will.

Problem Solving Compared to Building on Strength

What's Wrong		What's Right
Problem Solving: What's the Problem?		*Building on Strength: What's Working?*
Choose the negative as the focus of inquiry	INITIAL FOCUS	Choose the positive as the focus of inquiry
Grounded in *theory* of what will work.	FOUNDATION	Grounded in your *actual* experience and history
Identification of the problem	INITIAL THRUST	Appreciating, valuing the best of what is
Analysis of problems, search for causes	METHOD FOR IMPROVEMENT	Envisioning what might be. Seeing the common ground of our vision
Learn new way; change; find new solution	PROCESS OF IMPROVEMENT	Build on what we already know how to do
Your behavior	WHAT CHANGES?	The conditions which nurture you at your best
Analysis of possible solutions	NARROWING THE POSSIBILITIES	Dialoguing what could be
Action Planning treatment	FOLLOW UP	Innovating what will be
An organization is a set of problems to be solved	ASSUMPTION	An organization is a mystery to be embraced
Analysis	STRATEGY	Synthesis
Apollo	MYTHOLOGY	Dionysus
Left	BRAIN FUNCTION	Right

The Building on Strength (BoS) Process

Building on Strength begins as a normal human conversation, aimed at discovering the best, highest points, of a person's life, organizational achievements, or community strengths. We may be naturally hesitant to brag, but if encouraged just a little, people jump at the chance to talk about their finest hours—the moments in which they and their colleagues were able to operate in top form. As people connect with examples from their own lives, they begin to realize that approaching issues from a positive direction may actually work; energy is released and hope grows. An interview forms the core of BoS, and we discuss the interview process at length on Page 14. The important thing to remember is that the interview constructs a story about life and its successes, and is not intended to uncover secrets or assess blame for failures. The interviews are inquiries into the stories of life forces which enable us to be our best.

Appreciative Inquiry is a *journey* during which *profound knowledge* of a human system at its *moments of optimal performance* is used to construct the *best and the highest future* of that system.

David Cooperrider

Five Phases:
Definition, Discovery, Dream, Design, Delivery

David Cooperrider and his colleagues at Case Western Reserve defined five phases in this journey, in a 1990 study, funded by United States Agency for International Development (USAID).

I. *What will we study? Who will we interview? How?*

The **Definition Phase** determines what you are going to explore and how you will do it. You develop project goals, including questions and an inquiry protocol, participation strategy, and project management structure.

The Definition Phase should be considered iterative. As you or your group moves through the working phases of BoS—Discovery, Dream, Design, Delivery—you may redefine your project goals, expand the inquiry protocol and modify other components of the project. We suggest you hold a loose reign on the project to accommodate the speed of change possible using these techniques, and to accommodate the depth of change we've come to expect in BoS.

Once you have defined your topic, the journey begins.

II. *What is your historical best?*
What conditions existed to make it so?

The **Discovery Phase** uses interviews to elicit energizing stories. Every question is positive. The interviewer seeks and highlights the conditions present in exceptional moments of optimal human, economic, or organizational performance and discovers the conditions necessary for the best to flourish. This parallels the search that Jim Collins, in his business masterwork *Good to Great,* describes as a search for truth, not truisms. Collins' research reveals that great companies continuously explore critical questions:

- What are we best at?

- Where does our passion lie?

- Where is the economic driver?

- What does the customer value?

- Where can we be unique?

An executive team can possess no greater skill than a never-ending search for the overlap between the three key elements: our best, our passion, and our economic driver. The leader's job in this search is this: first, to ensure that the right people are on the executive team, and second, to create a team which has an ongoing dialogue to refine their discovery of the best.

III. *What could our best be?*
What might our best look like if we really built on it?

The **Dream Phase** asks participants to share images of what their organization could look, be, feel, and function like if the exceptional moments became the norm. The future becomes apparent from the revelations in the interviews. Just as a sculptor searches for beauty in the block of stone, participants search for what works well in their world. In the world of work, the dream may be called a compelling strategic focus or intent, or a powerful purpose or vision. Appreciative Inquiry practitioners have come to call this vision a provocative proposition. For more on provocative propositions, see Page 19.

IV. *What are the enabling conditions that fostered the best?*
How can we enhance and expand them?

The **Design Phase** builds a dream future grounded in the organization's positive past and the best of the present. Participants articulate and begin to agree on principles which produce conditions for them at their best. These are then used to guide changes in the organization's culture, structure and systems. Based on these principles, participants develop the steps necessary to lead change.

V. *How do we grow the enabling conditions to foster our best?*
    How do we actualize our proven potential by implementing and
    fine-tuning the enabling conditions?

The **Delivery Phase** suspends traditional planning, monitoring, and implementation strategies. Instead, the participants and the organization evolve into the preferred future. Experience tells us that building the best gets in the blood and the bone. It is iterative. Some have called it "positive protest" or "positive subversion." The ever-emerging insights from a BoS process reflect change itself. Like the great adventure of every human life, the adventure changes you, not the long-range plan.

Conditions for Success:

BoS requires integrity in the process. The system you wish to change must be included in the process from the start. We mean that if you want your organizational departments to work better together, you need to interview across functional lines and involve employees in decisions that will be made. If you want to improve visitor or audience services, or patient care, you'll need to hear their message loud and clear. Leaders attempting to use affirmative techniques within the organization, must positively model the desired behavior.

Most people need to envision change before they behave differently. Like the basketball coach attempting to replace the missed foul shots with nothing-but-net in the mind of his star player, the vision, or provocative proposition, needs to be in the minds and hearts of the volunteers, staff, board, and the organization's community.

During the interview process people usually experience something all too unfamiliar at work: validation and support. Telling stories of success and listening to those of others frequently taps into the very human need to connect with and understand one another. Real communication is based on understanding and trust, not technology, memos, or speeches.

The efficiencies imagined from e-mails, memos, plans, and policies give way to narrative communications: storytelling, face-to-face conversations, and well-designed forums. Decisions take longer in the beginning, but efficiencies are regained in the implementation phases. The organization and its members will begin to act differently towards one another, and that difference transforms each person in the organization and the organization itself. When organizational members share a common vision and truly understand one another, work can be, and is, accomplished at greater speed—sometimes much greater—with few or no unintended consequences.

The information for successful change comes from the people who will be making the change.

Consultants (internal or external) require a particular set of skills and knowledge in order to lead the BoS process.

- Facilitating skills for large groups
- Design and in-depth interview skill
- The ability to synthesize data into core themes
- Positive, constructive life-view

How to Start:

People exploring Building on Strength are at the start of something big. It seems clear that deficit-based change methods leave a lot to be desired. Many people immediately *get* the idea that knowledge-based organizations are human-centered. If you are intrigued, you'll find "how-to" suggestions in the remainder of this book. As you begin, keep in mind:

1. Start small. Debrief a project or event using BoS methods. Gain confidence and skill.

2. Don't forget problem solving. We are not suggesting you replace your problem solving skills with BoS skills. Rather, enhance your repertory with BoS skills.

3. Right people. If your institution has the wrong people on the bus or they are in the wrong seats, you will find major challenges creating positive change with BoS or any other change strategy.

4. The leader of the organization's primary responsibility is getting the right team and supporting the conditions that enable them to do their best.

Conducting a Positive Interview[1]

Workplace surveys and interviews traditionally are conducted with the idea of uncovering some "guarded truth" that the interviewee is reluctant to share. The interviewer may be viewed with suspicion. The interviewee wants anonymity. In contrast, the BoS interview usually leads to a positive interviewer/interviewee rapport through both its storytelling format and the positive questions.

Guidelines for BoS Interviews

Interviews can be conducted by pairing people or interviewers may be appointed.

- Pair with someone you do not know or would like to know better.
- Twenty to sixty minutes are usually needed for each personal interview.
- Choose a location where you both feel comfortable.
- The interviewer captures key words and phrases.
- The interviewer asks a set of prepared questions in sequence.
- If necessary, additional questions are used to encourage the interviewee.
- Let the interviewee tell his or her story. Refrain from giving yours. Your turn will come.
- Listen attentively. Be curious about the experience, the feelings, and the thoughts. Allow for silence.
- Have fun.
- Switch roles.

---

1. Guidelines, key characterizes, and synthesis for interviews adapted from Wakins & Mohr, pp.101/105.

- At the end of the two interviews, take some time to talk to your partner about what the interview was like for each of you. (This may be skipped if an interviewer is conducting multiple interviews.)

Key Characteristics of a BoS Interview

- The interview seeks to illuminate incidents and examples of people at their best.

- The interview reveals personal experiences and creates empathy, excitement, and commitment between the interviewer and the interviewee.

- Intense focus by the interviewer's listening leads to the experience of being fully heard and understood—a desirable effect from deep sharing takes place.

- The interviewer asks generative questions, cues, and guides the interview. The interviewer asks questions without interrupting the storyteller.

- Belief, rather than doubt, is the proper stance. The trust that develops from simply listening with interest contributes a major positive effect to the process.

- Stories, not necessarily facts, are being shared. The interviewer seeks details to understand the interviewees unique individual expression of the world.

- When negatives arise, the interviewer attempts to redirect back to the positive, to define a positive counterpoint, or postpones.

- The interview has two purposes:

  1. Articulation of the best, specifically and with passion.

  2. Identification of the conditions which enabled and nurtured the best.

Generic Interview Questions:

- *Best Experience*

   What is the best vacation you've ever experienced?

   When were you a good friend?

   What is the best celebration you ever planned or attended?

   When were you at your best on a work project?

   When was this organization at its best?

- *Values*

   What do you value most about yourself—as a worker, friend, parent, child, spouse?

   What do you value most when you are feeling best about your work?

   What do you value most about your organization?

   What is the single most important contribution of your life?

   What do you value most about being a member of your family, church, organization?

- *Wishes*

   What do you *really* want?

   What do you hope to achieve in this workshop, job, project, organization?

Specific Interview Questions:

Individual career development

- Describe a time in your life when you worked at your best.

- What gives you the greatest joy, satisfaction and renewal in life?

- Whom do you deeply admire and why?

- What is the most exceptional thing you've done in your life? In the last 3 months?

- What first attracted you to work in this field? What excited you?

- What were your initial experiences? When in your work have you felt most alive, most affirmed in your commitment to being a part of this type of work?

Improving an exhibition process in a museum

- Describe a time when working on an exhibit when you were at your best.

- What constitutes the best museum exhibit for you?

- What constitutes the best museum exhibit for your organization?

Improving teamwork across departments

- Describe the best team you know.

- Describe the best team involving people from different parts of the organization. What happened? What did you do? See? Feel? Experience?

Strengthening partnerships

- When have you seen a collaboration really work?

- What were the conditions that supported the collaboration?

- What makes us successful when we are at our best as a strategic partner?

Shaping the institution's future

- Tell of a time when this organization was at its best.

- Imagine this organization as the employer of choice in our community and the employer of choice in our industry. What does it look like? What are we doing more of? Less of? (Dream Phase)

Conflict resolution

- Describe the most constructively handled conflict you've witnessed. What did you do? Feel? See?

Becoming a learning organization

- Describe deep insights or learning that occurred at work. What happened? What did you experience?

Improving customer satisfaction

- Tell the story of the most delighted customer you ever met. What made that person delighted? What did you do? What did they do? What did your organization do?

- As a person working here, tell the story of the time you were able to serve/satisfy a customer to the absolute best of your ability.

Creating new products, services, or processes

- Tell the story of you at your best during the creation of a new product, service, or process and how it benefited the organization, what you learned, how you helped.

Interview Synthesis[2]

The interviews result in data requiring synthesis. The stories and quotes embody personal and organizational values and may reveal themes. Values and themes in turn reveal principles driving enabling conditions. Interviewers, individually and in small groups, will want to tease apart and clarify:

1. What do we, or I, look like at our best? What is the common ground we see at our best?

2. What are the enabling conditions?

3. What future was revealed or expressed?

Stories

- The most compelling stories that came from this interview.

Quotes

- The most quotable quotes that came from the interview.

Values

- Individual values evident from the interview.

- Organizational values evident from the interview.

Themes

- Themes appear from the ideas and qualities people report in their stories when they are energized, creative, at their best.

- Themes become the foundation for imagining the organization if the exceptional moments uncovered in the interviews became the norm.

- Examples of themes that sometimes emerge

  - Being the best

  - Acting with integrity

---

2. Guidelines, key characterizes, and synthesis for interviews adapted from Wakins & Mohr, pp.101/105.

- Recognizing deep imprints our work has on people
- Collaboration
- Teamwork
- Appreciating one another
- Building a sense of common ownership
- Establishing common ground for action

Provocative Propositions: Creating a Vision for Change

According to David Cooperrider, provocative propositions describe an ideal state of circumstances to foster conditions that create the possibility to do more of what works best. Whew! A rather long-winded sentence, but you get the message.

The purpose of provocative propositions is to keep the potential for your best at a conscious level. They remind you of what is best in the organization, and in yourself. They come from your stories, grounded in your history and tradition. Building on Strength provides every mind in the organization an opportunity to envision what could make the extraordinary possible on a daily basis.

Provocative propositions build a vocabulary of what is best and how to enable it. Using this vocabulary changes our minds and our behaviors individually and collectively. Every small step in the direction of creating conditions for enabling the best nurtures the growth of the best, which creates victorious, rather than a vicious cycle.

To create a Provocative Proposition:

1. Find examples from the best (from the Dream Phase).

2. Determine what circumstances, or enabling conditions, made the best possible (in detail).

3. Take the stories and envision what might be. Write an affirmative statement (a provocative proposition) describing the idealized future as if the conditions were already in existence.

To write the proposition, apply "what if" to all the common enabling themes which emerged from the interviews. Then write affirmative present-tense statements incorporating common themes.

Once written, test the proposition. Can you answer the following questions affirmatively?

1. Does it stretch, challenge or innovate?

2. Is it grounded in examples?

3. Is it what we want?

4. Will people defend it or get passionate about it?

5. Is it stated in affirmative, bold terms and in present tense, as if it were already happening?

Example: All of us perform at our best because each of us cares deeply about each other. Our caring shows up when we go out of the way to listen and understand one another's histories, families, talents, and aspirations.

A Practical Process Example Worksheet

1. CEO and executive team select area of inquiry.

   What?

   Who?

   When?

2. CEO, executive team or a subset facilitates the process.

   Who?

   How?

   When?

3. CEO and executive team introduce BoS to the institution.

   Who?

   How?

   When?

4. Conduct Interviews.

    Who will interview?

    Who will be interviewed?

    What questions?

    When?

5. Interviews synthesis.

    Who?

    When?

6. Present draft synthesis to institution.

    Who?

    When?

7. Dream Phase

8. Provocative Propositions

Definition Phase I: Life and Career Coaching

What will we explore?
How?

The **Definition Phase** determines what you are going to explore and how you will do it. The interviewer helps the interviewee develop personal goals through questions and an inquiry protocol.

Purpose: To learn enough about the person being interviewed to define the area you will explore and how you will do it.

Inquiry Protocol for BoS Interviews

- Pair with someone you do not know or would like to know better.
- Twenty to sixty minutes are usually needed for each personal interview.
- Choose a location where you both feel comfortable.
- The interviewer captures key words and phrases.
- Let the interviewee tell his or her story. Refrain from giving yours. Your turn will come.
- Listen attentively. Be curious about the experience, the feelings, and the thoughts. Allow for silence.
- Have fun.
- At the end of the two interviews, take some time to talk to your partner about what the interview was like for each of you.

Notes:

Discovery Phase II: Life and Career Coaching

What is your historical best?
What conditions existed to make it so?

Purpose: The Discovery Phase elicits life-energizing stories and understanding of the conditions present in exceptional moments. The interview is intended to reveal what the person is best at and what they are most passionate about. Later, you will consider where the economic engine resides. What are the perspectives, attitudes, feelings, and state of being in the individual which enabled their best to emerge?

1. The interviewee

    • list several times in your life when you were at your best at work (any work) or life. List times when you were extraordinary, times when you felt most appreciated, successful and engaged, times when you were at your peak and you felt most alive and involved.

2. The interviewer

    • asks the interviewee to describe one of the events on their list
    • encourages details and specifics
    • allows for silences
    • listens attentively, curiously
    • keeps notes on key words and phrases
    • list the questions which seem best to draw out the interviewee on the topic of his work life.

3. Together:

- Identify the conditions which enabled, encouraged, or supported you at your best: what conditions inside you (focus, attitudes, beliefs, emotions, knowledge, etc.) and what conditions around you (other people, works setting, mission, goals, etc.)

Notes:

Sample Questions: Life and Career Coaching

- Select six to eight times in your life when you were at your best.

- What is the most exceptional thing you've done in your life? In the last 3 months?

- Describe a time in your life when you worked at your best.

- What gives you the greatest joy, satisfaction and renewal in your life?

- Whom do you deeply admire and why?

- What first attracted you to work in your field?

- What were your initial experiences?

- When in your work have you felt most alive, most affirmed in your commitment to being a part of this type of work?

Notes:

Dream Phase III: Life and Career Coaching

What could your best be?
What might your best look like if we really built on it?

The **Dream Phase** asks participants to share images of what their life and work could look, be, feel, and function like if the exceptional moments became the norm. The future becomes visible through the articulation apparent from the revelations in the interviews. Just as a sculptor searches for the beauty in the block of stone, the participants search for what works well in their world.

1. The interviewee

    • Begins to develop a outline, then a sketch, then a masterwork of what their life or life work might look like, be, feel, function like.

2. The interviewer

    • Reveals in detail what he/she heard during the interviewer's questions: stories, learnings, implications, wishes, values, quotes, themes.

3. Together

    • Because a relationship has been created, the interviewer and interviewee build on what has been revealed to create one or more written visions of the interviewee's potential future.

    • Test, consider the vision against four criteria:

        1. Does the proposition stretch, challenge, or innovate?

        2. Is it grounded in real-life examples?

        3. Is it what you want? Are you passionate about it?

        4. Is it stated in affirmative, bold, present tense terms, as if it were already happening?

Notes:

Design Phase IV: Life and Career Coaching

What are the enabling conditions that fostered the best?
How can we enhance and expand them?

The **Design Phase** builds a dream future grounded in the person's positive past and the best of the present. Participants articulate and begin to agree on the conditions which enabled them at their best. Understanding these conditions helps develop clarity around the person's career plans. From understanding these conditions, participants can develop steps necessary to change or confirm career and life activity.

Together the interviewer and interviewee answer the questions below, eventually in writing.

What are the enabling conditions that fostered the best?	How can we enhance and expand them?

Notes:

Delivery Phase V: Life and Career Coaching

How do we grow the enabling conditions?

The **Delivery Phase** asks the participants to think through and identify the steps necessary to evolve into the preferred future, and then to implement them.

Notes:

Definition Phase I: A Project

What will we explore?
How?

The **Definition Phase** determines what you are going to explore, with whom, and how you will do it. You develop project goals, including questions and how to ask them, participating strategy, and a project management structure.

Inquiry Protocol for BoS Interviews

- Form a group of people interested in your topic.

- Appoint a time keeper, note taker, and facilitator.

- Choose a location where you feel comfortable.

- Decide on simple, positive questions to ask about the topic.

- If necessary and natural, additional questions can be asked.

- Everyone, and particularly the note taker, captures key words and phrases.

- Let the speaker tell his or her story.

- Listen attentively. Be curious about the experience, the feelings, and the thoughts. Allow for silence.

- Have fun.

- At the end of the interview, take some time to talk about what the interview revealed.

Notes:

Discovery Phase II: A Project

What is your historical best?
What conditions existed to make it so?

Purpose: The Discovery Phase seeks to elicit energizing stories and to under-stand the conditions present in exceptional moments. The interview is intended to reveal when the organization was at its best, where the passion for the issues lie. Later, you will consider where economic engines reside. You are looking for clues to the conditions enabling the best of organizational work. What are the structures, people, systems, culture, sanctions or other condi-tions that allowed the best work to be accomplished?

1. The interviewee:

    -   list several times in your organization life when you were at your best at work, as it relates to the issues your have chosen to explore. List times when you were extra-ordinary, times when you felt most appreciated, successful and engaged—times when you were at your peak and you felt most alive and involved.

Notes:

2. The interviewer

    -   asks the interviewee to describe one of the events on their list.

    -   encourages details and specifics.

    -   allows for silences.

    -   listens attentively, curiously.

    -   keeps notes on key words and phrases.

    -   list the questions which seem best to draw out the interviewee on the topic of his work life.

Notes:

3. Interviewers:

    - After collecting the stories from the interviewees in an organizational inquiry, identify recurring themes which emerge. Themes are core ideas or qualities that people report as most energizing, most creative, most present at their best. These themes become the foundation for imagining what the organization would be if the exceptional moments uncovered in the interviews became the norm.

    - Dialogue to determine the most powerful themes.

    - Examples of themes:

        - acting on integrity.

        - recognizing the affects of our work on the lives of others.

        - appreciation of the work of others.

        - building from common ownership.

Notes:

Sample Interview Questions

Improving our exhibition process in a museum

- Describe the times when working on an exhibit when you were at your best.
- What constitutes the best museum exhibit for you?
- What constitutes the best museum exhibit for your organization?

Improving teamwork across departments

- Describe the best team you know.
- Describe the best team involving people from different parts of the organization. What happened? What did you do? See? Feel? Experience?

Strengthening partnerships

- When have you seen a collaboration really work?
- What are the conditions evident which supported the collaboration?
- What makes us successful when we are at our best as a strategic partner?

Shaping the institution's future

- Tell of a time when this organization has been at its best.
- Imagine it as the employer of choice in our community and the employer of choice in our industry. What does it look like? What are we doing more of? Less of? (Dream Phase)

Conflict resolution

- Describe the most constructively handled conflict you've witnessed. What did you do? Feel? See?

Becoming a learning organization

- Describe deep insights or learning that occurred at work. What happened? What did you experience?

Improving customer satisfaction

- Tell the story of the most delighted customer you ever met. What made that person delighted? What did you do? What did they do? What did your organization do?

- As a person working here, tell the story of the time you were able to serve/satisfy a customer to the absolute best of your ability.

Creating new products, services, or processes

Tell the story of you at your best during the creation of a new product, service, or process and how it benefited the organization, what you learned, how you helped.

Dream Phase III: A Project

What could your best be?
What might your best look like if we really built on it?

The **Dream Phase** asks participants to share images of what the work could look, be, feel, and function like if the exceptional moments became the norm. The future becomes visible through the articulation apparent from the revelations in the interviews. Just as a sculptor searches for the beauty in the block of stone, the participants search for what works well in their world. What is the organization being called or propelled to do? What are the most exciting possibilities for the organization? What is the inspiration?

1. The interviewers

    *   Begin to develop an outline, then a sketch, then a masterwork of what the work might look like, be, feel, function like. The interviewers reveal, in detail, what they heard during the interviewees' stories, learnings, implications, wishes, values, quotes, themes.

    *   Build on what has been revealed, to create one or more written visions of the work, improved.

    *   Test, consider, the vision against four criteria:

        1. Does the proposition stretch, challenge, or innovate?

        2. Is it grounded in real-life examples?

        3. Is it what you want? Are you passionate about it?

        4. Is it stated in affirmative, bold, present tense, terms, as if it were already happening?

Notes:

Design Phase IV: A Project

What are the enabling conditions that fostered the best?
How can we enhance and expand them?

The **Design Phase** builds a dream future grounded in the organization's positive past and the best of the present. Participants articulate and begin to agree on the conditions which enabled them at their best. Understanding these conditions helps to develop clarity around the organization's future. From understanding these conditions, participants can develop the steps necessary to change or confirm organizational activity.

What are the enabling conditions that fostered the best?	How can we enhance and expand them?

Notes:

Delivery Phase V: A project

How do we grow the enabling conditions?

The **Delivery Phase** asks the participants to think through and identify the steps necessary to evolve into the preferred future, and then to implement them.

Notes:

References:

Bolles, Richard Nelson, *What Color Is Your Parachute? A Practical Manual for Job-Hunters & Career-Changers*, Ten Speed Press; ISBN: 1580083412; 2002 edition (December 2001).

Buckingham, Marcus and Curt Coffman, *First Of All, Break All The Rules: What the World's Greatest Managers Do Differently*, Simon & Schuster; ISBN: 0684852861; 1st edition (May 1999).

Collins, James C. and Jerry I. Porras, *Built to Last: Successful Habits of Visionary Companies*, Harper Business, 1997, ISBN: 0887307396.

Collins, Jim, Good *to Great: Why Some Companies Make the Leap and Others Don't*, HarperCollins, 2001, ISBN: 0066620996.

Cooperrider, David and Diana Whitney, *Collaborating for Change: Appreciative Inquiry*, Peggy Holman and Tom Devane, Editors, Berritt-Koehler Communications, San Francisco, 1999.

Hammond, Grant Tedrick, *The Mind of War: John Boyd and American Security*, Smithsonian Institution Press, 2001, ISBN: 1560989416.

Hammond, Sue Annis, *The Thin Book of Appreciative Inquiry*, Thin Book Pub Co; ISBN: 0966537319; 2nd edition (November 1998).

Hammond, Sue Annis and Cathy Royal, Editors, *Lessons From the Field: Applying Appreciative Inquiry* (Revised Edition) Thin Book Publishing Co.; ISBN: 0966537335; (September 15, 2001).

Holman, Peggy and Tom Devane, Editors, *The Change Handbook: Group Methods for Shaping the Future*, Berrett-Koehler; ISBN: 1576750582; 1st edition (July 1999).

Watkins, Jane Magruder and Bernard J. Mohr, *Appreciative Inquiry*, Jossy-Bass/Pfeiffer, San Francisco 2001. ISBN: 0-7879-5179-X

http://www.qm2.org

www.ingramcontent.com/pod-product-compliance
Lightning Source LLC
Chambersburg PA
CBHW021049180526

45163CB00005B/2343